Cyber Security Defence in Depth

About the Author

```html

A distinguished veteran of the UK Armed Forces, the author seamlessly bridges the gap between military discipline and cutting-edge cybersecurity practices. With over two decades of hands-on experience in Communications and IT, they possess a deep understanding of the complexities surrounding digital security. Their authoritative insights stem from a career committed to protecting organizations from ever-evolving threats, making their writing both credible and compelling to readers seeking clarity in a complex field.

Throughout their extensive career, the author has collaborated with a variety of stakeholders, including local and central government departments across the UK, showcasing their versatile skill set in cybersecurity. This breadth of experience has honed their ability to develop and implement robust controls tailored to various organizational needs. Their practical and strategic insights, grounded in real-world applications, empower organizations to fortify their defenses against a rapidly changing threat landscape, offering readers a wealth of knowledge to draw upon.

Holding a wealth of knowledge complemented by advanced education in Communications and IT, the author's academic background enriches their writing and guides their analytical approach to cybersecurity. Their journey as a writer was shaped by the desire to demystify cybersecurity concepts for a broader audience. This book, "Cyber Security Defence in Depth," serves as both a concise guide and a comprehensive reference, born from a passion to educate and elevate awareness about the critical importance of cybersecurity in our increasingly digital age.

In this book, the author's accessible and engaging writing style reflects their commitment to making complex topics relatable to all readers. They draw upon a plethora of real-world experiences, employing anecdotes and practical examples to illuminate key concepts. This approach not only enhances understanding but also fosters a genuine connection with the audience, ensuring that the nuances of cybersecurity resonate on a personal level.

As a passionate advocate for cybersecurity awareness, the author envisions a future where every individual is equipped with the knowledge necessary to navigate digital threats confidently. Their mission is to continue sharing insights and best practices that drive a collective improvement in cybersecurity resilience. With aspirations to engage in public speaking and consulting, they aim to inspire future generations to prioritize cybersecurity, ultimately contributing to a more secure digital landscape for all.

```

Table of Contents

Chapter 1: Introduction to Defence in Depth

(3) - 1.3 Overview of Layers in Defence

Chapter 2: Theoretical Framework

Chapter 3: Threat Landscape

Chapter 4: Network Architecture

Chapter 5: Perimeter Security

(1) - 5.1 Firewalls and Their Configurations

(2) - 5.2 Intrusion Detection and Prevention Systems (IDPS)

(3) - 5.3 Virtual Private Networks (VPNs)

Chapter 6: Endpoint Security

Chapter 7: Application Security

Chapter 8: Data Protection

Chapter 9: Security Monitoring and Incident Response

(1) - 9.1 Security Information and Event Management (SIEM)

(2) - 9.2 Incident Detection and Analysis

(3) - 9.3 Incident Response Planning

Chapter 10: Cloud Security

(1) - 10.1 Challenges and Considerations

(2) - 10.2 Securing Cloud Services

(3) - 10.3 Compliance and Regulatory Concerns

Chapter 11: Identity and Access Management

(1) - 11.1 Authentication and Authorization Models

(2) - 11.2 Role-Based Access Control (RBAC)

(3) - 11.3 Multi-Factor Authentication Mechanisms

Chapter 12: Physical Security

Chapter 13: Security Governance and Compliance

Chapter 14: Future Trends in Cyber Security

(1) - 14.1 Emerging Technologies and Their Implications

(2) - 14.2 AI and Machine Learning in Security

(3) - 14.3 The Role of Automation

Chapter 15: Case Studies and Real-World Applications

Chapter 16: Conclusion and Next Steps

(1) - 16.1 Recap of Key Concepts

(2) - 16.2 Continuing Education in Cyber Security

(3) - 16.3 Building a Career in Defence in Depth

Chapter 1: Introduction to Defence in Depth

1.1 Definition of Defence in Depth

Defence in Depth is a critical concept in the field of cybersecurity, one that emphasizes a strategic layering of security measures to safeguard an organization's information and assets. This multifaceted approach means that if one layer of defense is breached, others remain to protect against potential threats. By employing several types of security controls across various points within a network, organizations can significantly reduce the risk of unauthorized access, data breaches, and other malicious activities. This layering can include a combination of physical security measures, firewalls, encryption, access controls, endpoint protection, and regular security assessments, all designed to work together to create a stronger security posture.

The philosophy behind Defence in Depth is rooted in the understanding that no single security measure is foolproof. Each layer serves as a critical part of a larger security framework, integrating diverse technologies and practices that form a comprehensive strategy for risk management. This holistic approach recognizes that threats can come from numerous directions and that relying on a single defense mechanism, such as a firewall or antivirus software, is insufficient. By interconnecting various security processes and technologies, organizations can create a more resilient infrastructure capable of absorbing and responding to attacks while maintaining operational continuity. It fosters a mindset that encourages holistic security thinking, enabling cybersecurity professionals to design environments that are adaptive, responsive, and capable of evolving alongside emerging threats.

In implementing a Defence in Depth strategy, cybersecurity professionals should focus on ensuring that each layer not only functions independently but also enhances and supports the others. This interconnectedness can lead to a more robust defense, where the failure of one layer does not compromise the entire system. An effective Defence in Depth model combines preventive, detective, and responsive measures, allowing organizations to stay one step ahead of cyber threats. One practical tip for cybersecurity professionals is to perform regular audits of security layers, ensuring that they are updated and functioning as intended, as a proactive measure against evolving threats.

1.2 Importance in Cyber Security

Defence in Depth is a crucial strategy in the world of cyber security, acting as a multi-layered defense system designed to protect sensitive data and critical infrastructure. By implementing multiple security controls throughout an organization's network, from the perimeter to the endpoint, this approach significantly mitigates risk. If one layer of defense is breached, others still stand in place to thwart intruders. This continuous stratification not only enhances the overall security posture but also creates a more resilient network capable of withstanding various types of cyber threats, whether they be external attacks or internal vulnerabilities. Security professionals need to understand the interplay of these layers, as each contributes uniquely to decreasing the likelihood of successful attacks, ensuring that a breach at any single point does not compromise the entire system.

The value propositions of Defence in Depth resonate powerfully with both security professionals and organizational leaders. For security practitioners, it offers a structured approach to thinking about security. By designing networks with multiple defensive strategies, professionals can articulate the rationale and necessity behind security investments. It fosters a proactive mindset where risks are anticipated and managed efficiently. From an organizational standpoint, implementing Defence in Depth translates directly to increased trust from clients and stakeholders, as it demonstrates a committed stance on data protection. Moreover, the financial implications are significant; while the upfront costs of establishing a multi-layered defense may seem daunting, the long-term benefits of preventing data breaches, which can be enormously costly, far outweigh these initial investments. This strategy not only protects the organization's assets but ultimately strengthens its reputation and market positioning.

Understanding the principles of Defence in Depth is essential for those looking to excel in cyber security roles. A practical tip for professionals is to regularly evaluate and update their security layers based on the evolving threat landscape. This includes conducting risk assessments and implementing new technologies as they emerge. Staying informed about the latest vulnerabilities and attack vectors allows professionals to adapt their strategies accordingly, ensuring their networks are fortified against the next wave of cyber threats.

1.3 Overview of Layers in Defence

In the Defence in Depth model, various layers work synergistically to fortify an organization's security posture. Understanding these layers—physical, technical, and administrative controls—helps in constructing a robust defense against potential threats. Physical controls encompass the tangible measures that protect an organization's assets, such as locks, surveillance cameras, and security personnel. These measures deter unauthorized access and provide environmental security, ensuring that critical systems are not compromised by physical intrusions. When developing network designs, it is essential to assess physical layouts and position essential hardware within secure areas to minimize risks.

Technical controls are the next layer, consisting of software tools and solutions designed to protect the network and its data. This layer includes firewalls, encryption, intrusion detection systems, and antivirus software. Each of these components serves a specific function; for instance, firewalls monitor incoming and outgoing traffic based on predetermined security rules, while encryption safeguards sensitive data from unauthorized access. It is crucial to integrate these technical controls effectively to create a multilayered defense that can detect and respond to cyber threats promptly. The efficacy of these controls often depends on maintaining regular updates and patches to defend against emerging vulnerabilities.

Administrative controls provide the third layer in this multifaceted defense strategy. These involve the policies and procedures established by the organization that govern security practices and user behavior. Administrative measures include user training, access control policies, and incident response plans. Ensuring employees understand their roles in the cybersecurity framework helps mitigate human errors, which are often the weakest link in security. When these three layers—physical, technical, and administrative—operate in concert, they create a complementary defense architecture. This layered approach ensures that if one control fails, others remain in place to protect critical assets. Therefore, it is vital to regularly evaluate and strengthen each layer of security to adapt to the ever-evolving threat landscape. By doing so, organizations not only protect their infrastructure but also cultivate a culture of security awareness among their staff.

Chapter 2: Theoretical Framework

2.1 Security Models and Theories

Understanding various security models is crucial for cybersecurity professionals aiming to create robust defense-in-depth strategies. The Bell-LaPadula model, for example, is a state machine model that focuses on maintaining the confidentiality of information. It does this through mandatory access control and employs the principle of no read up, no write down, ensuring that users cannot access data at a higher classification level than their own. This model is particularly applicable in environments where data confidentiality is paramount, such as government and military operations. On the other hand, the Biba model emphasizes data integrity, preventing users from writing to higher integrity levels, hence maintaining data purity. These models serve as foundational theories in developing layered security approaches, reinforcing the notion that multiple security measures can protect vital assets more effectively than singular solutions. The interplay of these models in a defense-in-depth strategy allows organizations to build an architecture that not only secures access but also maintains the trustworthiness of the information being processed.

Contemporary cybersecurity theories have evolved, influenced by the complex, ever-changing landscape of technology and cyber threats. One significant theory is the Cyber Kill Chain, which offers a structured approach to understanding and mitigating cyber attacks. This model outlines the stages an attacker goes through, from reconnaissance to execution, providing professionals with insights to detect and interrupt attacks at various points. Another influential framework is the MITRE ATT&CK framework, which catalogs adversary tactics, techniques, and procedures based on real-world observations. This knowledge empowers professionals to anticipate potential threat actions and implement defenses accordingly. Additionally, concepts like Zero Trust have gained traction, positing that no entity, whether inside or outside the network, should be automatically trusted. Instead, verification is required at every stage of a transaction. Integrating these contemporary theories into network design not only reinforces security measures but also creates a dynamic environment where defenses can evolve with emerging threats.

Applying insights from both established security models and contemporary theories enriches the design of networks with defense in depth in mind. A practical tip for cybersecurity professionals is to regularly evaluate and update defensive measures against the backdrop of these models and theories. This ensures that security protocols are aligned with current best practices, reinforcing an organization's protective posture against both known and unknown threats. Utilizing a layered approach based on these principles means not only dressing vulnerabilities but transforming the overall approach to cybersecurity into a resilient and proactive defense mechanism.

2.2 Risk Management Principles

Risk management principles are foundational to any effective strategy related to cyber security, especially when implementing a Defence in Depth approach. These principles emphasize the importance of understanding the context in which an organization operates, the assets it seeks to protect, and the potential threats it faces. At the core, risk management involves identifying risks, assessing their potential impact, and deciding how to address them. By taking a systematic approach, cybersecurity professionals can ensure that multiple layers of security controls are not only deployed but optimized to work in concert, thereby enhancing the resilience of the network. This layered defense strategy is designed to protect against different types of threats and incidents, ensuring that if one layer is breached, additional layers still provide protection. The concept of Defence in Depth encourages ongoing evaluation and adaptation, as threats constantly evolve, and so must the strategies to mitigate them.

Creating a roadmap to assess and prioritize risks within an organization involves several critical steps. First, cybersecurity professionals must conduct a thorough risk assessment. This process begins with asset identification, recognizing what critical data, systems, and processes require protection. Once the assets are identified, potential threats and vulnerabilities can be examined, allowing teams to determine the risk each poses. After mapping out risks, it is essential to prioritize them based on the likelihood of occurrence and the severity of their impact. This prioritization process helps in allocating resources efficiently, ensuring that the most significant risks are addressed first. Developing a structured approach for risk assessment not only aids in securing networks but also fosters a culture of continuous improvement, where security measures are regularly reviewed and updated in response to changing threats. Incorporating regular risk assessments and updates into the organizational routine empowers teams to maintain a robust Defence in Depth strategy.

2.3 Layered Security Concepts

The necessity of establishing multiple barriers to threats through layered security approaches cannot be overstated in today's complex cyber landscape. Layered security, often referred to as defense in depth, extends beyond just relying on a single protective measure. Each layer of security serves a distinct purpose, working collaboratively to safeguard sensitive information and critical infrastructure from potential breaches. By integrating various security mechanisms—such as firewalls, intrusion prevention systems, and endpoint security measures—organizations can effectively reduce their attack surface and limit the likelihood of successful penetration. This methodology recognizes that no single system is foolproof; hence, combining protective strategies means that if one layer fails, others will still stand firm against threats. For cyber security professionals, designing networks with this multi-layered approach in mind is essential for ensuring a robust security posture.

Evaluating the effectiveness of layered security implementations involves a thorough understanding of various techniques and metrics. One effective method is to conduct regular penetration testing, simulating real-world attacks to identify vulnerabilities across the different layers. This proactive approach is invaluable because it not only highlights weaknesses in the defense mechanisms but also provides insights on areas that require strengthening. Additionally, security audits and compliance assessments can be instrumental in evaluating existing systems, ensuring that each layer is aligned with best practices and organizational policies. Metrics such as the number of detected threats, response times, and incident severity can inform security teams about the effectiveness of their layered defenses. An iterative process of continuous improvement allows professionals to adapt their strategies based on findings from these evaluations, ultimately enhancing the overall security architecture.

Integrating a layered security strategy demands not just a technical solution, but also a cultural shift within an organization toward security awareness. Training employees to recognize potential threats and respond appropriately adds yet another layer of defense. Remember that cyber threats are constantly evolving; therefore, staying informed about the latest trends and technologies is vital. Regularly updating security protocols, investing in advanced threat detection tools, and fostering a culture of vigilance among team members are all critical practices. As you design and implement layered security strategies, continuously seek innovative ways to reinforce these protective measures, ensuring your defenses remain resilient against an ever-changing threat landscape.

Chapter 3: Threat Landscape

3.1 Common Vulnerabilities and Exploits

Commonly exploited vulnerabilities in systems and applications often stem from misconfigurations, outdated software, and inherent flaws in the code. One of the most significant vulnerabilities is the exploitation of unpatched software, where known security loopholes can be targeted by attackers to gain unauthorized access. For instance, the infamous Heartbleed bug in OpenSSL showcased how a simple oversight could allow attackers to siphon sensitive data from server memory. The impact of such vulnerabilities can be profound, leading to data breaches, financial loss, and a loss of trust from clients and customers. Understanding these vulnerabilities is crucial for cybersecurity professionals aiming to design resilient networks using a defense-in-depth approach.

Analyzing past incidents provides invaluable context for understanding the current threat landscape. Take the Target data breach in 2013, where attackers exploited weak third-party vendor access, resulting in the theft of millions of credit card numbers. This incident highlighted the need for a comprehensive security strategy that includes not only internal defenses but also scrutinizes third-party vulnerabilities. Another pertinent case is the Equifax breach of 2017, which occurred due to the failure to patch a known vulnerability in Apache Struts, affecting over 147 million people. These incidents illustrate not only the severe repercussions of exploited vulnerabilities but also emphasize the importance of continual monitoring and vulnerability management as vital components of a robust cybersecurity strategy.

To effectively mitigate risks associated with common vulnerabilities, cybersecurity professionals must adopt a proactive approach. Regular software updates and thorough patch management can dramatically reduce the risk of exploitation. Moreover, integrating automated tools for vulnerability scanning and employing threat intelligence can help organizations stay a step ahead of potential attackers. Continuous security training for all employees is equally essential, reinforcing the idea that everyone plays a role in safeguarding the network. This layered defense ensures that even if one security measure fails, others will stand firm, reinforcing the fortifications of a well-designed network.

3.2 Understanding Attack Vectors

Attack vectors are the various pathways or methods that cybercriminals use to infiltrate systems and networks. Understanding these vectors is crucial in the development and planning of Defense in Depth strategies, which aim to create multiple layers of security to protect assets. Each attack vector presents unique vulnerabilities, and by identifying them, cybersecurity professionals can implement protective measures at various levels. This multi-layered approach adds complexity for potential attackers, making it harder for them to succeed in breaching defenses. The significance of attack vectors lies in their ability to inform the design and implementation of security architectures, ensuring that organizations can anticipate potential threats and build resilience against them.

As technology evolves, so do the attack vectors that cybercriminals exploit. For instance, as more organizations adopt cloud computing and mobile technologies, attackers are increasingly targeting these environments through vulnerabilities specific to them. This evolution means that cybersecurity professionals must adopt a proactive approach to defense. Rather than merely responding to threats after they occur, understanding how attack vectors are changing allows for the anticipation of potential attacks. By continuously analyzing how these vectors evolve, cybersecurity experts can enhance their defensive strategies, enabling them to stay one step ahead of adversaries. This could involve regularly updating software to patch vulnerabilities, training employees to recognize phishing attempts, or employing advanced threat detection tools that adapt to new attack patterns.

Incorporating a dynamic understanding of attack vectors into security planning not only strengthens defenses but also fosters a culture of security awareness within organizations. A practical tip for cybersecurity professionals is to perform regular threat modeling exercises. These exercises can help identify potential attack vectors relevant to your organization and assess the effectiveness of existing defense mechanisms. By staying informed about the latest trends in cyber threats and continuously updating security protocols, teams can significantly bolster their Defense in Depth strategies.

3.3 Emerging Cyber Threats

As technology advances, so do the threats that organizations face in the cyber landscape. New and evolving threats, such as ransomware, supply chain attacks, and sophisticated phishing schemes, pose serious challenges to security professionals. Ransomware attacks have escalated in frequency and complexity, targeting not just critical infrastructure but also smaller enterprises that may lack robust cybersecurity measures. These threats highlight the importance of understanding attack vectors and the potential implications for business continuity and data integrity. Supply chain attacks, such as those witnessed in high-profile cases, demonstrate how third-party vulnerabilities can be exploited to gain access to sensitive information. As attackers become more adept at leveraging emerging technologies, including artificial intelligence and machine learning, the potential for sophisticated attacks increases, making it crucial for organizations to remain vigilant and proactive in their defenses.

To effectively counter these emerging threats, adapting Defence in Depth principles is essential. This strategy involves layering security controls to create multiple barriers against attackers. By implementing a mix of preventive, detective, and responsive controls, organizations can enhance their resilience against evolving cyber threats. For example, combining firewalls, intrusion detection systems, and endpoint protection creates a multifaceted defense that can prevent unauthorized access and detect breaches early. Additionally, organizations should consider integrating threat intelligence into their security posture. This allows them to stay informed about new vulnerabilities and emerging threats, ensuring that defenses are continuously updated to meet these challenges. Regular training and awareness programs also play a key role in preparing staff to recognize and respond to phishing attempts and other social engineering tactics that are increasingly being used by cybercriminals.

Chapter 4: Network Architecture

4.1 Designing Secure Networks

Best practices for designing networks with integrated security focus on creating layers of defense right from the beginning. This approach, commonly referred to as defense in depth, emphasizes that no single security measure is sufficient on its own. Instead, it's crucial to build multiple layers of security to protect sensitive data and assets. Every layer should encompass various strategies, from physical security controls to technical safeguards. Implementing network segmentation is one fundamental practice that can enhance security. By dividing the network into smaller segments, it becomes more difficult for attackers to move laterally within the environment. Each segment can apply specific security controls tailored to the risks associated with that particular area, effectively containing potential breaches. Regularly updating and patching systems also plays a critical role in keeping vulnerabilities at bay. Establishing a policy for timely updates and assessments helps ensure that no system slips through the cracks, enabling a robust security posture.

Hardware and software considerations are vital in securing network architectures. When selecting hardware, it's important to choose devices that come with built-in security features, such as firewalls, intrusion detection systems, and secure boot mechanisms. These features provide an extra layer of protection against unauthorized access and reduce the attack surface. From a software standpoint, network security solutions should employ a mix of proactive and reactive measures. Firewalls, antivirus, and intrusion prevention systems can armor the network against external threats, while logging and monitoring software can provide insights into potential security incidents. It's also crucial to evaluate and choose software based on its compatibility and integration capability with existing security measures. Proper training on software solutions ensures that teams are prepared to respond effectively to incidents, fostering a culture of security awareness throughout the organization.

Staying informed about the latest security technologies and threat landscapes significantly aids in designing more secure networks. Engaging with the cybersecurity community through workshops, seminars, and online forums can provide valuable insights and practical tips for enhancing network security. Regular security audits can help identify vulnerabilities within the network architecture before they are exploited. Additionally, fostering collaboration between various departments within an organization can lead to a more comprehensive understanding of security needs and allow for the implementation of more effective measures. One practical tip is to always evaluate both current and future needs when designing a network, aiming for scalability and flexibility, which will allow the network to adapt to evolving threats and business requirements.

4.2 Segmentation Strategies

Network segmentation is a fundamental concept in cybersecurity that involves dividing a larger network into smaller, more manageable sections. By creating these discrete segments, organizations can significantly improve their security posture. The principles underlying this approach include minimizing the attack surface, containing breaches, and enhancing overall network visibility. When a network is segmented, the potential damage from a security incident can be contained within a smaller area. This containment limits the impact on the entire network and helps prevent unauthorized access to critical systems. Furthermore, segmentation allows for tailored security policies that can be applied to specific segments based on their unique requirements and risk profiles. This targeted approach not only strengthens security but also improves compliance with industry regulations, which often mandate specific controls for sensitive data.

There are various techniques that can be utilized for effective network segmentation, including physical, logical, and virtual segmentation. Physical segmentation involves the use of separate hardware devices such as routers and switches. This approach is highly secure but can be cost-prohibitive and complex to manage. Logical segmentation, on the other hand, uses software to create separate networks within the same hardware, enabling distinct security policies for different segments. VLANs (Virtual Local Area Networks) are a popular example of logical segmentation, allowing traffic to be segmented based on roles, teams, or functions while sharing the same physical infrastructure. Virtual segmentation combines elements of both physical and logical methods, leveraging virtualization technologies to create isolated environments while optimizing resource use. Each of these techniques can fit well within a Defense in Depth strategy, enhancing layered security by ensuring that if one segment is compromised, the attacker's movement is restricted, limiting their ability to access other segments.

When employing segmentation strategies, it is crucial to consider how they integrate with a Defense in Depth framework. This approach requires multiple security layers, each providing distinct protections and responses to threats. Network segmentation can act as one of these layers, working alongside firewalls, intrusion detection systems, and endpoint protection. The interaction between these components improves resilience against attacks by adding barriers that an attacker needs to cross, making unauthorized access much more difficult. Moreover, proper monitoring and logging of traffic between the segments enhance situational awareness and incident response capabilities. Regularly reviewing segment boundaries and maintaining clear communication between network segments significantly boosts security measures. As a practical tip, cybersecurity professionals should consider incorporating segment-based firewall rules and inspect inter-segment traffic diligently to maintain a robust defense against potential breaches.

4.3 Implementation of DMZs

Demilitarized Zones, or DMZs, play a crucial role in enhancing network security by acting as a buffer zone between an internal network and untrusted external environments such as the internet. This segmented area allows organizations to host external-facing services, such as web servers or email gateways, while minimizing the risk of an attacker directly accessing the internal network. By isolating these services, DMZs create a controlled environment where traffic can be monitored, and potential threats can be mitigated before they impact critical assets. The architecture of a DMZ typically involves multiple layers of security features, such as firewalls and intrusion detection systems, which collectively work to prevent unauthorized access and safeguard sensitive information. Understanding the strategic placement and purpose of a DMZ is essential for any cybersecurity professional looking to bolster their network defense mechanisms.

Implementing DMZs effectively within a Defence in Depth framework involves a multi-layered security strategy that incorporates various defensive measures. The creation of a DMZ should not only focus on physical placement but also on logical segmentation of network traffic. Each layer of defense must work cohesively, allowing for thorough inspection and control of data flows entering and exiting the DMZ. It is vital to configure firewalls to enforce strict access control rules, which determine what traffic is permitted from the external environment to the DMZ and subsequently to the internal network. Additionally, deploying intrusion prevention systems (IPS) within the DMZ will help actively analyze traffic patterns and prevent threats in real-time. When combined with other layers of security, such as endpoint protection and employee training, the DMZ becomes a powerful component within the larger security architecture.

To ensure that DMZs are not only implemented but also optimized for effectiveness, regular audits and updates of security policies are necessary. Monitoring and logging traffic that passes through the DMZ allows for ongoing assessment of its integrity. Incident response plans should also include specific protocols related to DMZ breaches or compromises, ensuring that organizations can react swiftly to incidents. Advanced threat detection mechanisms can further enhance the security posture of a DMZ by using machine learning and behavior analysis to identify anomalous activities. As you design networks with a foundations of Defence in Depth, remember that a well-structured DMZ is not simply about adding another layer of security, but about creating a resilient architecture that can adapt to the evolving threat landscape. Focusing on the integration of security principles and continuously adapting to new threats is key to making the most out of your DMZ implementation.

Chapter 5: Perimeter Security

5.1 Firewalls and Their Configurations

Firewalls serve as critical gatekeepers in perimeter security, functioning to control the flow of data between internal networks and untrusted external sources. Their essential roles include packet filtering, which examines incoming and outgoing packets to determine whether they should be allowed or blocked based on predefined security rules. State inspection, another vital function, tracks the state of active connections and ensures that only legitimate packets pertaining to those sessions are permitted through. Additionally, many modern firewalls support deep packet inspection, which inspects the payload of packets for malicious content, providing an extra layer of security. Configuring firewalls involves establishing comprehensive rules that govern acceptable traffic patterns based on factors such as IP addresses, protocols, and ports. Best practices for firewall configuration include regularly updating rules and policies to adapt to evolving threats, segmenting networks to limit attack vectors, and implementing logging and monitoring to detect suspicious activity promptly.

There are several types of firewalls, each with its own strengths and weaknesses. Packet-filtering firewalls are effective for simple setups and provide a basic level of security by examining header information. However, they lack the contextual awareness necessary for dealing with sophisticated threats. Stateful firewalls offer improved security by maintaining context about active sessions, making them better suited for more complex environments. On the downside, they can be resource-intensive, which may affect performance under high traffic loads. Next-generation firewalls (NGFWs) incorporate additional layers of functionality, such as intrusion prevention systems and application awareness, enabling them to analyze traffic more deeply. While these firewalls offer improved security, they can also be more complicated to configure and require constant management to remain effective. Understanding these various types allows network architects to select the most appropriate firewall for their requirements, balancing the need for security with performance and manageability.

Designing networks with defense-in-depth in mind means incorporating multiple layers of security controls, and firewalls play a significant role within this paradigm. Continuous assessment of firewall effectiveness, along with a commitment to learning about new vulnerabilities and emerging technologies, can enhance an organization's security posture. Utilizing a multi-faceted approach that combines firewalls with other security measures like intrusion detection systems and endpoint protection will provide a more robust defense against potential breaches. Regular training and awareness programs for IT staff and end users can also greatly improve overall security, ensuring that everyone understands the role of firewalls and other security appliances, and remains vigilant against threats. Operators should regularly review firewall configurations and adjust rulesets based on changing environments, traffic patterns, and emerging threats to achieve optimal network resilience.

5.2 Intrusion Detection and Prevention Systems (IDPS)

Intrusion Detection and Prevention Systems (IDPS) play a critical role in cybersecurity by actively monitoring network traffic and system activities for suspicious behavior. They can identify potential security threats and take action against them in real-time, significantly reducing the risk of data breaches and various attacks. IDPS can be categorized into two main types: intrusion detection systems (IDS) which focus on recognizing and signaling alerts for potential breaches, and intrusion prevention systems

(IPS) that not only detect these threats but also take immediate steps to block them. The detection capabilities of IDPS range from signature-based methods, which rely on known threat patterns, to anomaly-based techniques that identify unusual behavior not previously cataloged. This multi-faceted approach allows security professionals to respond swiftly to incidents, minimizing damage and maintaining the integrity of systems.

A layered security approach helps to mitigate risks effectively, and integrating IDPS into this framework is vital for enhancing overall security posture. One strategy involves positioning the IDPS at multiple critical points across the network, creating several layers of oversight that can detect and neutralize threats. For example, implementing an IDPS in front of firewalls can provide an additional layer of scrutiny, allowing for preemptive measures before any malicious traffic reaches sensitive systems. Furthermore, integrating IDPS with other security solutions, such as firewalls and endpoint protection systems, facilitates real-time data sharing and threat intelligence collaboration. This synergy allows security teams to gain a more comprehensive view of their environments and improve response times during potential incidents.

Effective integration of IDPS goes beyond mere placement; it requires a thorough understanding of network architecture and potential vulnerabilities. Cybersecurity teams should ensure that IDPS configurations align with the organization's risk management strategy, adjusting their settings based on the types of data processed and assets protected. Regular updates and testing of IDPS are essential to maintain its efficiency against evolving threats. Moreover, training staff on interpreting IDPS alerts is crucial, ensuring they can act decisively in response to detected incidents. By establishing a robust IDPS strategy as part of a defense-in-depth architecture, organizations can better safeguard their resources and enhance their overall security resilience.

5.3 Virtual Private Networks (VPNs)

Understanding how Virtual Private Networks (VPNs) enhance secure communication over untrusted networks is crucial for security professionals. A VPN creates a secure tunnel through which data travels, encrypting information to prevent unauthorized access. This is particularly important when using public Wi-Fi networks where data exposure risks are heightened. By masking the user's IP address, a VPN also provides a layer of anonymity, preventing malicious actors from tracking online activities. VPNs employ protocols like OpenVPN and IPSec, which can vary in strength and efficiency. It's essential to choose a protocol that matches the security needs of your network while considering performance metrics. Furthermore, it's beneficial to recognize the limitations of VPNs. They protect the data in transit, but if devices are compromised before the data enters the VPN tunnel, threats may still be prevalent.

Best practices for implementing and managing VPNs should focus on integrating them into a broader security strategy. Ensure that the VPN solution is scalable to accommodate growth in users and devices as organizations evolve. Regularly monitor and audit VPN usage to identify potential risks or unauthorized access and adjust policies as needed. Strong authentication methods, such as multi-factor authentication, help ensure that only legitimate users gain access to the network. Keep the software and protocols updated to defend against vulnerabilities. Establish clear usage policies to inform employees about safe browsing habits while using VPNs and the importance of protecting their credentials. Security training can significantly reduce risks associated with human error, which often exploits the vulnerabilities of even the most robust technical defenses. Always have a contingency plan in place; understand the potential attack vectors that could bypass VPN protections.

A practical tip for ensuring the effectiveness of your VPN setup is to regularly conduct penetration testing or simulations to assess the strength of your overall security posture. This proactive approach highlights weak points within the VPN configuration and network defenses, allowing for timely improvements before a real attack occurs. Remember that utilizing a VPN is not a silver bullet; it should be part of a layered security approach that includes firewalls, intrusion detection systems, and security policies to create a defense-in-depth architecture.

Chapter 6: Endpoint Security

6.1 Anti-Malware Solutions

Anti-malware solutions play a crucial role in safeguarding endpoints from a multitude of threats that can disrupt operations and compromise sensitive information. In an increasingly digital world, where cyber threats are evolving rapidly, the importance of a robust anti-malware strategy cannot be overstated. Each endpoint, whether it's a personal computer, laptop, or mobile device, represents a potential entry point for malicious software. Malware can lead to data breaches, ransom demands, and significant financial losses. By investing in effective anti-malware solutions, organizations can create a first line of defense that not only detects and removes malware but also prevents future infections by recognizing patterns indicative of malicious behavior. Moreover, integrating these tools within a defense-in-depth strategy enhances an organization's overall security posture, ensuring that if one layer fails, others are in place to respond.

Evaluating various anti-malware tools reveals a diverse landscape of options, each with its own strengths and weaknesses. Some tools excel in traditional signature-based detection, effectively identifying known threats through regularly updated databases. However, as cybercriminals often employ new techniques to bypass these defenses, heuristic and behavior-based approaches are increasingly emphasized. These methods analyze the behavior of software to identify suspicious activity that may not yet be cataloged. Furthermore, many modern solutions are moving to cloud-based architectures, allowing for more efficient analysis and quicker updates compared to local solutions. When assessing the effectiveness of anti-malware solutions, it's vital for cybersecurity professionals to consider not just the detection rates of individual tools, but also their scalability, ease of management, and integration capabilities with existing security infrastructures. The right tool should complement other security measures without overwhelming resources and should facilitate a proactive rather than solely reactive approach to cybersecurity.

When selecting anti-malware solutions, it can be beneficial to look for products that offer centralized management consoles, allowing for streamlined oversight of multiple endpoints. Continuous learning and adapting are essential in the cyber security field. Therefore, engaging in regular security assessments and staying updated on the latest malware trends and countermeasures will further enhance the effectiveness of your chosen solutions. Ultimately, choosing the right tools is just as important as implementing them in a way that fosters an adaptive and resilient security environment.

6.2 Security Patching and Updates

Regular patch management plays a critical role in maintaining endpoint security by addressing vulnerabilities that can be exploited by cyber threats. Keeping systems updated with the latest security patches helps protect sensitive data and maintains the integrity of the network. Failure to apply patches in a timely manner can lead to significant security breaches, as attackers often target unpatched software to gain unauthorized access. By ensuring that all software is regularly reviewed and updated, organizations can minimize the attack surface and bolster their defense mechanisms. The agility with which patches are applied can significantly impact overall security posture, making effective patch management an indispensable element of an organization's security strategy.

Establishing a robust framework for update deployment and compliance is essential to streamline the patch management process. Organizations should create clear policies that define how updates are identified, tested, and deployed. The framework should incorporate automation tools that can facilitate the timely and consistent rollout of updates across all endpoints. In addition, regular audits and compliance checks can ensure that all systems remain up-to-date, allowing security teams to quickly identify and rectify any discrepancies. Moreover, clear communication channels should be established within the organization to ensure that all stakeholders are aware of upcoming updates and their necessity, fostering a culture of security awareness and proactive defense against potential vulnerabilities.

Prioritizing patches based on the severity of vulnerabilities is another key aspect of an effective patch management strategy. Not all updates carry the same level of risk, and organizations can benefit from risk assessment practices that help prioritize which patches to deploy first. This strategic approach allows cyber security professionals to focus on the most pressing threats while still maintaining a steady cadence of updates across the environment. It is important to remember that timely execution of these processes can significantly enhance the resilience of a network, reducing the likelihood of successful attacks and ultimately safeguarding critical assets and sensitive information.

6.3 Endpoint Detection and Response (EDR) Tools

EDR tools are essential in the modern cybersecurity landscape, designed to proactively detect and respond to threats targeting endpoints such as desktops, laptops, and servers. One of the significant features of EDR tools is their ability to provide continuous monitoring and detection of suspicious activities, utilizing advanced analytics, machine learning, and behavioral analysis. This capability allows organizations to identify anomalies that may indicate a potential breach or malicious activity, often before any significant damage occurs. Additionally, EDR tools offer real-time response capabilities, enabling security teams to contain threats swiftly, isolate compromised endpoints, and remediate issues with minimal disruption to operations. This seamless blending of detection and response streamlines the investigation process, providing security analysts with a rich context of events leading up to an incident, thereby improving incident response time and accuracy.

Implementing EDR effectively requires a strategic approach, especially within a Defense in Depth framework. This layered security strategy emphasizes the importance of using multiple defensive mechanisms to protect sensitive data and systems. When integrating EDR, organizations should ensure that the tool complements existing security measures, such as firewalls, intrusion detection systems, and antivirus solutions. This can involve configuring EDR to share threat intelligence with other security layers and utilizing the insights gained from EDR analyses to bolster overall security policies. Moreover, proper deployment often includes defining clear roles and responsibilities for incident response teams, which are crucial for ensuring effective communication and coordinated responses to threats across different levels of security management. Training and familiarization with EDR tools are also vital, as skilled personnel are necessary to maximize the effectiveness of these solutions and adapt their use to evolving threats.

Using EDR tools as part of a comprehensive Defense in Depth strategy not only enhances an organization's ability to detect and respond to threats but also creates a culture of proactive security awareness among employees. Regular updates to EDR systems ensure protection against the latest threats, and continual refinement of detection algorithms improves accuracy over time. For cybersecurity professionals, understanding the nuances of EDR implementation will significantly enhance their capability to design networks that are resilient to attacks. A practical tip is to conduct simulated attack scenarios using EDR capabilities to test the responsiveness of your incident response plans and fine-tune them based on real-world insights gained during these exercises.

Chapter 7: Application Security

7.1 Secure Software Development Lifecycle (SDLC)

The principles of secure coding are vital for creating software that not only functions effectively but also protects sensitive information from malicious threats. Secure coding involves applying best practices and guidelines to mitigate vulnerabilities throughout the development process. This is especially significant in the context of the Software Development Lifecycle (SDLC), a structured approach that enables developers to build software in a disciplined and repeatable manner. The importance of a robust SDLC cannot be overstated; it helps in systematic identification and management of security risks, ensuring that security becomes an integral part of the development process rather than an afterthought. Adopting secure coding principles within the SDLC framework fosters a culture of security awareness that enhances the overall resilience of applications against cyber threats, facilitating the development of secure software products.

Integrating security practices throughout each phase of the SDLC is crucial for building an effective defense against potential security flaws. In the planning phase, stakeholders should identify security requirements by performing risk assessments and defining security objectives. During the design phase, employing threat modeling can help identify potential attacks and vulnerabilities, allowing developers to create architectural designs that inherently account for security risks. As development proceeds, employing secure coding practices and conducting peer code reviews ensures that security considerations are maintained. Testing phases should include dynamic and static analysis tools that specifically target security vulnerabilities to ensure that weaknesses are identified and remediated before deployment. Even in the deployment phase, maintaining security through processes such as vulnerability assessments and patch management ensures that the software remains secure throughout its lifecycle. By embedding security at every stage of the SDLC, organizations can significantly reduce the likelihood of security breaches and create robust applications that align with the principles of defense in depth.

Consider incorporating automated security testing tools alongside regular manual tests for a more comprehensive security strategy. These automated tools can provide continuous feedback, enabling your team to address issues early in the development process, thus ensuring a more secure software product upon release.

7.2 Code Review Practices

Code reviews play a crucial role in identifying vulnerabilities early in the development process. By systematically analyzing the code written by developers, teams can catch security issues before they make their way into production. This proactive approach allows for immediate corrections, helping to prevent vulnerabilities that could be exploited by malicious actors. Engaging in regular code reviews encourages team collaboration and knowledge sharing, as more experienced developers can mentor newer team members, reinforcing good security practices. Moreover, the feedback loop created through code reviews not only enhances the code quality but also fosters a culture of security awareness within the team, making security a shared responsibility rather than an afterthought.

Various methodologies and tools exist to facilitate effective code reviews. Pair programming, for instance, allows two developers to work together, instantly identifying potential issues as they write code. This collaborative method promotes real-time feedback, reducing the chances of serious vulnerabilities slipping through. Peer reviews, on the other hand, involve having another developer evaluate the code after it has been written. Tools like GitHub and GitLab provide platforms where code can be peer-reviewed seamlessly. Advanced static analysis tools can automate parts of the code review process, checking for known vulnerabilities and adherence to coding standards, thus streamlining the review while accentuating areas that need further human inspection. Integrating these methodologies and tools not only improves code quality but also strengthens the overall security posture of the network design.

An effective practice in code reviews is to include criteria that specifically address security concerns. Establishing checklists tailored for security vulnerabilities can ensure that crucial aspects are not overlooked. For example, items like input validation, authentication measures, and access controls should be scrutinized during reviews. By embedding security requirements directly into the review process, teams can enhance their ability to build resilient systems. Additionally, fostering an environment where developers feel encouraged to ask questions and seek clarification during reviews can lead to more thorough and insightful discussions around security, ultimately strengthening the defense-in-depth approach.

7.3 Vulnerability Assessment Techniques

Vulnerability assessment techniques play a critical role in identifying and remediating potential security weaknesses within applications. The process begins with mapping the application's architecture to understand how various components interact. This mapping allows security professionals to pinpoint areas typically prone to vulnerabilities, such as interfaces, data storage, and configuration settings. Performing a thorough analysis often involves checking for known vulnerabilities, especially those listed in databases like the Common Vulnerabilities and Exposures (CVE). Additionally, conducting thorough code reviews can unveil vulnerabilities that automated tools might overlook, providing a comprehensive view of a system's security posture.

The effectiveness of automated tools versus manual assessment is a nuanced topic. Automated tools offer rapid assessments and are invaluable for scanning large numbers of applications efficiently; they can quickly detect common vulnerabilities and flag them for remediation. However, relying solely on automation can result in missed context-specific issues that require a human eye to discern. Manual assessments play an essential role in addressing this limitation by providing the necessary depth for understanding the complex interactions within the application. Skilled security professionals bring critical thinking and experience, allowing them to identify subtle security flaws that automated tools might overlook. Combining both approaches typically yields the best results, fostering a more resilient application environment.

Investing time in both techniques not only enhances the security assessment process but also strengthens the overall defense posture of the network. Implementing a multi-layered security strategy, where both automated tools and manual assessments are utilized cohesively, can significantly reduce the surface area for potential attacks. Understanding how and when to apply these techniques can make all the difference in safeguarding applications against evolving threats.

Chapter 8: Data Protection

8.1 Encryption Standards and Practices

Understanding key standards for encryption is crucial for anyone working in the field of cybersecurity. Various encryption standards, such as AES (Advanced Encryption Standard), RSA (Rivest-Shamir-Adleman), and SHA (Secure Hash Algorithm), serve as the bedrock for securing sensitive information. AES, for instance, is widely recognized for its efficiency and robustness, making it the go-to choice for encrypting data in transit and at rest. RSA, on the other hand, plays an essential role in public key infrastructure, allowing secure key exchanges. SHA algorithms are vital for ensuring data integrity by creating unique hash values. Adopting these standards not only ensures compliance with regulatory requirements but also builds trust among users by safeguarding their sensitive data against unauthorized access. It's important to keep abreast of any updates or changes to these standards, as cyber threats continually evolve, necessitating enhancements in encryption practices.

While selecting the right encryption mechanism, professionals face the challenge of balancing encryption strength with system performance. The stronger the encryption, the more computational resources are required, which can lead to slower system performance. This becomes particularly critical in environments where data needs to be processed quickly, such as in real-time applications or high-frequency trading systems. Cybersecurity professionals must assess the specific needs of their network, taking into account factors like the sensitivity of the data, the potential risks involved, and the capabilities of the hardware being used. Often, implementing a tiered encryption approach can be effective; using lightweight encryption for less sensitive data while reserving stronger encryption methods for the most critical information. By finding this balance, organizations can maintain a secure environment without significantly compromising operational efficiency.

Security is not just about implementing technology; it's also about ongoing evaluation and adaptation. Regularly reviewing encryption practices and their effectiveness can lead to better security postures. As new threats emerge, staying informed about advancements in encryption technology and trends in cyber threats is vital. Cybersecurity professionals should engage in continuous learning and consider participating in forums and workshops to exchange knowledge and strategies. This proactive stance ensures that your encryption practices not only meet current standards but also anticipate future developments in the cybersecurity landscape.

8.2 Data Loss Prevention (DLP) Strategies

Data Loss Prevention (DLP) strategies are essential in today's digital landscape where sensitive information is at constant risk of unauthorized exposure. Organizations must implement a combination of technologies and processes designed to safeguard data, especially personal and confidential information, from unintended sharing or intentional theft. These strategies typically involve endpoint security measures, network security tools, encryption, and employee training programs focused on data handling best practices. DLP tools can monitor data in use, in motion, and at rest to ensure comprehensive protection. For example, an organization might deploy software that scans emails and attachments for sensitive information, automatically flagging or blocking any outgoing messages that contain unencrypted personal data or proprietary business insights. Additionally, integrating behavior analytics can help identify anomalies in user activity that may indicate potential data breaches, allowing security teams to respond swiftly.

When examining the integration of DLP within the broader security landscape, it's essential to recognize that DLP is not a standalone solution but rather a critical component of a multilayered defense strategy. Effective cybersecurity relies on the interaction between various security measures, including firewalls, intrusion detection systems, and identity and access management. DLP technologies must be configured to work seamlessly alongside these systems to provide real-time insights and enhance breach detection capabilities. For instance, when a DLP solution identifies a potential data leakage event, it can trigger alerts in conjunction with other security systems, allowing for immediate response actions. As cyber threats evolve, incorporating threat intelligence into DLP strategies also enhances their effectiveness by ensuring the organization is prepared against the latest tactics employed by cybercriminals.

To maximize the effectiveness of DLP strategies, fostering a culture of security awareness within the organization is crucial. Regular training sessions that emphasize the importance of data protection and provide practical tips on identifying phishing attempts can empower employees to act as the first line of defense. Simple measures, such as not sharing passwords, recognizing suspicious emails, and understanding the implications of data mishandling, can significantly reduce the risk of data loss. Additionally, organizations should establish clear policies regarding data access and sharing to ensure everyone understands their role in protecting sensitive information. By intertwining technological solutions with human elements in your DLP strategy, you build a robust framework that effectively minimizes data exposure risks.

8.3 Access Control Mechanisms

Access control mechanisms serve as a critical barrier in protecting sensitive information and systems from unauthorized users. These methods ensure that only authenticated and authorized individuals can access certain data or resources. Various access control methods include mandatory access control (MAC), discretionary access control (DAC), role-based access control (RBAC), and attribute-based access control (ABAC). MAC enforces a policy where access rights are regulated by a central authority based on multiple levels of security. On the other hand, DAC allows owners of resources to make decisions regarding who can access what. RBAC streamlines access by associating permissions with roles rather than individual users, which is particularly useful in larger organizations. ABAC enhances flexibility by granting access based on attributes of users, resources, and the environment. Understanding and implementing these access control types is essential for securing data effectively in modern networks, as they provide the foundational guidelines that dictate who can interact with what in a system.

Effective access controls are pivotal in supporting the Defence in Depth strategy, which emphasizes a layered approach to security. This strategy acknowledges that any one control can be bypassed, hence the necessity for multiple overlapping controls. Implementing robust access control measures enhances security at multiple layers in the network. For instance, it starts at the perimeter where firewalls and intrusion detection systems may filter traffic. Once inside the network, access controls limit what authenticated users can see and do, further thwarting potential breaches. Furthermore, by integrating access controls with monitoring systems, organizations can track and log access attempts, adding another layer of defense. If an attacker gains initial access, having strong access control mechanisms can prevent them from moving laterally across the network, thereby mitigating the overall impact of a security breach.

As security professionals, it is crucial to regularly assess and update access control measures in response to evolving threats and organizational changes. Knowledge of these mechanisms not only aids in the design of secure networks but also in compliance with regulations that mandate data protection. Regular audits of access controls can reveal discrepancies or outdated permissions that might expose vulnerabilities, ultimately safeguarding the integrity of sensitive data. Incorporating these practices will not only bolster security but also enhance operational efficiency, making it an integral aspect of responsible cybersecurity management.

Chapter 9: Security Monitoring and Incident Response

9.1 Security Information and Event Management (SIEM)

SIEM systems play a vital role in modern cybersecurity by centralizing the collection and analysis of security data. These systems gather logs and security-related documentation from various sources such as servers, domain controllers, firewalls, and other network devices. A key functionality is real-time monitoring, which enables security teams to detect and respond to threats promptly. SIEM solutions aggregate data from multiple environments — on-premises, cloud, and hybrid — applying analytics to identify anomalies that could indicate a security incident. This analysis often employs machine learning and behavioral analysis to uncover hidden patterns or suspicious activities that might go unnoticed during routine monitoring. Additionally, SIEM systems provide a comprehensive view of the organization's security posture, assisting in compliance reporting by generating logs and reports that demonstrate adherence to regulatory standards.

To ensure that a SIEM system is effective in threat detection, configuring it according to best practices is essential. One primary consideration is the relevance and volume of data collected; focusing on high-value logs and avoiding data overload is crucial for efficient analysis. Setting up alerts tailored to the environment allows security teams to prioritize responses based on the severity and context of potential threats. Regular maintenance is also critical; this includes conducting updates to the system, fine-tuning alerts, and ensuring that the rules and correlation logic remain aligned with the evolving threat landscape. Integrating threat intelligence feeds can enhance the SIEM's capabilities by augmenting the detection of known threats. Additionally, periodic audits and assessments of the SIEM configuration help to identify any gaps and ensure that it continues to meet the organization's security needs.

Implementing these practices not only optimizes the performance of SIEM systems but also strengthens the overall security framework of an organization. Among the practical tips is ensuring that you have a well-defined incident response plan that can be activated once potential threats are detected. This preparation allows you to analyze logged incidents effectively and can significantly reduce response times, minimizing the potential damage from attacks. Regular training and simulations for your security team on how to utilize the SIEM tools effectively can further enhance operational readiness and adaptability to any emerging threats.

9.2 Incident Detection and Analysis

Timely detection of security incidents is crucial for minimizing the impact on an organization. There are several methodologies that cybersecurity professionals can implement to enhance the efficiency of incident detection and resolution. Utilizing automated monitoring tools can significantly shorten the time it takes to identify irregular patterns or suspicious activities within network traffic. These tools use algorithms and machine learning techniques to analyze vast amounts of data in real-time, allowing for rapid response to potential threats. Furthermore, establishing a robust incident response plan is essential. This plan should include clear procedures for identifying, classifying, and addressing security incidents. Regular training exercises can help to ensure that all team members understand their roles in this process and can react swiftly when an incident occurs.

Correlating events and logs is another essential component in analyzing potential threats effectively. Security information and event management (SIEM) systems play a vital role in this process by aggregating data from various sources, including firewalls, intrusion detection systems, and application logs. Professionals should focus on designing their logs with comprehensibility and relevance in mind, ensuring that critical events are easily accessible and actionable. By developing correlation rules that focus on identifying relationships between seemingly disparate incidents, cybersecurity teams can gain deeper insights into potential security breaches. This not only speeds up threat detection but also aids in understanding the tactics, techniques, and procedures employed by adversaries.

Incorporating threat intelligence into your incident detection and analysis framework provides another layer of defense. By leveraging external and internal threat intelligence feeds, cybersecurity professionals can stay informed of the latest vulnerabilities, attack methods, and emerging threats. Integrating threat intelligence with correlation techniques enhances the ability to predict and mitigate risks before they escalate into full-blown incidents. Therefore, continuous learning and adaptation to new threats are crucial elements for developing a resilient security posture. Regularly updating and refining correlation rules and detection methodologies based on the evolving threat landscape ensures that responses remain relevant and effective.

9.3 Incident Response Planning

An effective incident response plan is essential for any organization looking to fortify its cybersecurity posture. Several critical components make up this plan. First and foremost is the identification of incident types, which should encompass a range of scenarios, including data breaches, ransomware attacks, and insider threats. This will help in tailoring the response procedures appropriately. Next, establishing clear roles and responsibilities is crucial; it allows team members to understand their specific tasks during an incident. Communication plans must also be outlined to ensure that information is disseminated properly both within the organization and to external stakeholders, taking care to deliver timely updates without compromising sensitive information. Furthermore, the plan should include a robust methodology for detecting and assessing incidents, which should guide how to identify abnormal activities and prioritize responses. Finally, the documentation of lessons learned after an incident is invaluable; this allows organizations to iterate on their response strategies continuously, aligning them with ever-evolving threats.

Training and simulations form the backbone of incident response preparedness. Regular and comprehensive training enables team members to familiarize themselves with the protocols established in the incident response plan. Without training, even the best-designed plans can falter when real incidents arise, as team members may react chaotically under pressure. Simulations, including tabletop exercises and live-fire drills, are critical in creating a realistic environment where staff can practice their responses. These exercises not only test the plan but also highlight gaps in knowledge or procedure that need addressing. The more realistic the simulation, the more effectively an organization can prepare for potential incidents and ensure that team members can execute their roles confidently and efficiently. Engaging in such proactive training helps to unify the incident response team, fostering collaboration and communication, which are vital during actual events.

Looking ahead, incorporating feedback mechanisms into both training exercises and real-world response situations is vital. Create a culture of continuous improvement by encouraging team members to contribute their insights on what worked well and what didn't. This process ensures that the incident response plan remains a living document, constantly evolving to meet new challenges. As cyber threats become more sophisticated and prevalent, organizations must remain agile in their responses, and ongoing training is the key to achieving this adaptability.

Chapter 10: Cloud Security

10.1 Challenges and Considerations

Cloud computing environments introduce a variety of unique security challenges that professionals must address. The migration of data and services to the cloud complicates the traditional perimeter-focused security model. One of the most significant issues is data visibility; once data is stored in the cloud, it can be hard to track and monitor where it resides, making it vulnerable to unauthorized access. Additionally, the shared responsibility model complicates security measures, as organizations must clearly understand their roles versus those of the cloud service provider. Misconfigurations, which are common in cloud settings, can expose sensitive information to threat actors. Attack vectors such as insecure APIs and vulnerabilities within cloud applications further elevate the risk landscape, demanding a multi-layered security approach that encompasses not just technical solutions, but also procedural safeguards and user education.

When it comes to identity management and data governance in the cloud, several critical considerations must be made. Establishing robust identity management is essential to ensure that only authorized users can access sensitive information. This includes implementing strong authentication methods, such as multi-factor authentication, and detail-rich user access controls. Without granular control over who accesses what, the risk of data breaches increases significantly. Data governance must also be prioritized; organizations need to define clear policies regarding data classification, storage, and sharing. This governance should include data encryption both at rest and in transit, as well as thorough auditing processes to maintain compliance with regulations. By investing in these identity management and data governance strategies, cyber security professionals can bolster the integrity and security of the cloud environment.

To enhance security posture when dealing with cloud technologies, remember to focus on continuous monitoring and assessment. Adopting automated tools can provide ongoing insights into security configurations and vulnerabilities, enabling quicker responses to potential threats. Regular training and awareness programs for employees can further cultivate a culture of security, ensuring that everyone plays a role in protecting sensitive data. Ultimately, the combination of solid identity management, thorough data governance, and proactive security measures will create a robust defense in depth for cloud-based resources.

10.2 Securing Cloud Services

Securing cloud services begins with understanding the best practices for configuration management and risk assessment. Configuration management ensures that all systems are consistently configured according to security policies. This includes maintaining documentation, automating deployments, and regularly auditing configurations to prevent misconfigurations, which are often a weak point in security. Implementing a version control system can greatly assist in tracking changes in configurations over time. While securing configurations is critical, risk assessment helps prioritize those configurations based on the potential threats and vulnerabilities faced. Risk assessments should be regular, looking for new threats like zero-day vulnerabilities or shifts in the threat landscape. A thorough risk assessment will include evaluating the current deployment of services, identifying sensitive data, and ranking risks based on their likelihood and impact. By maintaining an ongoing cycle of assessing risks and managing configurations, organizations can adapt their security posture to emerging challenges.

The role of third-party service providers in cloud security cannot be underestimated. Many businesses rely on service providers for critical functions, such as data storage, application hosting, and infrastructure management. However, while third-party services can enhance agility and cost-effectiveness, they also introduce new security risks. It is essential to assess the security measures implemented by these providers, including their compliance with industry standards like ISO 27001 or GDPR. Understanding the shared responsibility model is crucial; while the cloud provider manages the security of the cloud, the customer must secure their data within it. Engaging in regular audits, obtaining security certifications, and ensuring transparency in security protocols can foster a stronger risk management relationship. Furthermore, establishing clear SLAs (Service Level Agreements) that detail security obligations can help safeguard against potential breaches. As organizations leverage third-party services, they must remain vigilant and proactive to minimize vulnerabilities.

For professionals working in cyber security, being aware of these practices not only fosters robust security architectures but also cultivates a culture of accountability. Regular training sessions aimed at both your teams and third-party personnel can ensure everyone understands the importance of their roles in maintaining security. A little investment in regular security training often pays dividends, as it equips all team members with the knowledge required to identify and mitigate threats effectively. Remember, cyber security is a collaborative effort, and only through shared diligence can organizations maintain a secure environment.

10.3 Compliance and Regulatory Concerns

Common compliance frameworks play a critical role in cloud security, particularly GDPR (General Data Protection Regulation) and HIPAA (Health Insurance Portability and Accountability Act). GDPR, which affects organizations operating in or offering services to EU citizens, emphasizes the protection of personal data and gives individuals greater control over their information. Businesses must implement stringent data processing and storage policies, ensuring that personal data is not only protected but that breaches are reported promptly. On the other hand, HIPAA governs how health information is handled and requires healthcare organizations and their business associates to maintain the confidentiality and integrity of health data. Compliance with these frameworks is not merely a checkbox exercise; these regulations require a deep understanding of how to apply security controls effectively while using cloud services.

Maintaining compliance while implementing cloud security measures involves integrating these regulatory requirements into every aspect of cloud architecture and operational practices. Organizations must adopt a comprehensive compliance strategy that aligns security measures with specific regulatory mandates. This includes leveraging encryption for data at rest and in transit to protect sensitive information, conducting regular audits, and ensuring that there is a clear incident response plan in position. It is crucial to educate all employees about compliance impacts and best practices since human error can often lead to regulatory breaches. Employing a defense-in-depth approach means layering security controls so that if one measure fails, others can still protect sensitive data, thereby ensuring ongoing compliance even amidst evolving threats.

For practical implementation, it is beneficial to use compliance management tools that can automate reports and alerts regarding your compliance status. These tools can provide insights and maintain logs of access and data usage, thus aiding in audits and assessments. Regularly revisiting both your cloud security posture and compliance requirements ensures that your organization stays ahead of any regulatory changes. Cybersecurity professionals should also engage in continuous learning and participate in training to comprehend the ever-changing compliance landscape, ensuring that the security frameworks designed remain robust against both compliance challenges and security threats.

Chapter 11: Identity and Access Management

11.1 Authentication and Authorization Models

Authentication and authorization are crucial elements in the field of cybersecurity, each serving a distinct but interrelated purpose. Key models such as XACML (eXtensible Access Control Markup Language) and OAuth play significant roles in shaping the architecture of security in applications and networks. XACML is primarily designed for defining access control policies. It allows organizations to express security policies in a standardized way that can be interpreted and enforced consistently across different systems. This model decentralizes decision-making by separating the policy enforcement from the policy decision point, which helps in managing complex environments where various services and resources might have differing access needs.

On the other hand, OAuth provides a method for users to grant third-party services limited access to their data without exposing their credentials. It does this by allowing the user to authorize the third party to act on their behalf without sharing passwords directly. This model is particularly useful in today's interconnected digital landscape, where different applications need to work together while maintaining user security and privacy. Understanding how to implement and integrate these models can enhance your ability to design robust security frameworks that enforce the principle of least privilege while offering a seamless user experience.

Understanding the distinction between authentication and authorization is critical for professionals working in cybersecurity. While authentication is the process of verifying the identity of a user or system, authorization determines what that authenticated entity can do. In simpler terms, think of authentication as the process of checking a person's ID to confirm their identity, while authorization is akin to managing access levels—deciding who can enter a particular room and what they can do once inside. A solid security framework must clearly delineate these processes to avoid vulnerabilities. As you design networks with defense in depth in mind, ensure that both aspects are not only secure but also clearly defined, thereby reducing the potential for unauthorized access and maintaining the integrity of your networks.

In practice, implementing both authentication and authorization effectively requires using best practices like multi-factor authentication (MFA) and role-based access control (RBAC). These practices can significantly enhance the security posture of your network by adding layers of verification and ensuring that users have access only to the information necessary for their roles. By focusing on these elements within your network design, you will not only strengthen defenses but also foster an environment of trust and secure interactions.

11.2 Role-Based Access Control (RBAC)

RBAC is a crucial strategy for managing user access and strengthening data security within organizations. It operates on the principle of assigning permissions based on users' roles rather than their individual identities, streamlining the access control process. This role-centric model not only simplifies the administration of user privileges but also ensures that employees only have access to the information necessary for their job functions. By grouping users into specific roles, organizations can implement permission sets that closely align with job responsibilities, thereby minimizing the risk of unauthorized access to sensitive data. This layer of security is vital in today's environment, where protecting data assets against internal and external threats is a top priority.

However, implementing RBAC comes with its own set of challenges. One significant hurdle is the initial mapping of roles to specific permissions, which requires a thorough understanding of organizational processes and job functions. This mapping is not a one-time effort; it must evolve as roles change and new systems are introduced. Regular audits are also necessary to ensure that the permissions granted remain relevant and that any outdated roles are updated or removed. Additionally, organizations may face resistance from employees who are accustomed to having more access than what RBAC permits. To address these challenges, best practices such as involving stakeholders during the role definition phase can lead to more effective implementation. Regular training and clear communication about the importance of RBAC help foster a culture of security awareness within the organization.

11.3 Multi-Factor Authentication Mechanisms

Multi-factor authentication (MFA) encompasses a variety of methods designed to enhance security by requiring multiple forms of verification before granting access. This process often combines something the user knows, like a password, with something they have, such as a mobile device or a token, and sometimes even something they are, like biometric data. The goal is to create layers of security that make it significantly harder for unauthorized users to gain access to sensitive information or systems. Examples of multi-factor authentication include SMS or email codes, authenticator applications that generate one-time codes, and biometric scans, such as fingerprints or facial recognition. By employing these mechanisms, organizations can effectively mitigate risks associated with password breaches, social engineering attacks, and other vulnerabilities that can compromise access control. The implementation of such diverse forms of MFA directly enhances the resilience of an organization's network architecture, ensuring that, even if one factor is compromised, additional verification is still required to breach security.

Implementing multi-factor authentication strategies can vary significantly across different organizational contexts, tailored to meet specific needs and risk profiles. In high-security environments, such as financial institutions, the use of MFA may be mandatory for all users, incorporating rigorous checks that often require biometric identification along with traditional credentials. Conversely, smaller companies with limited resources may adopt simpler forms of MFA, like SMS codes or one-time passwords, which balance user convenience with necessary security measures. Regardless of scale, organizations must assess their unique operational requirements and potential threats to design an effective MFA strategy. Furthermore, the successful application of these multifactor strategies often necessitates training employees on the importance of MFA and the potential risks of lax security practices. Developing clear policies and providing user-friendly tools can help ensure adoption and reduce the likelihood of user resistance, thus fostering a culture of security awareness throughout the organization. This multifaceted approach is critical in designing secure networks, as it forms part of a broader defense-in-depth strategy that layers various controls to protect sensitive data.

As cyber threats continue to evolve, the landscape of multi-factor authentication is also shifting, with emerging technologies enhancing traditional methods. For instance, the integration of machine learning can help identify anomalous login attempts that may indicate a breach, allowing for real-time alerts and responses. Staying informed about these advancements is essential for cybersecurity professionals striving to fortify networks effectively. To remain agile in this ever-changing field, organizations should regularly review and update their authentication mechanisms, ensuring they address new vulnerabilities and leverage new technologies. Emphasizing the use of adaptive authentication, where the level of scrutiny can change based on factors such as location or behavioral anomalies, allows for a more nuanced approach that balances user experience with security. Implementing and maintaining robust multi-factor authentication is not merely a checkbox on a security list; it is an ongoing commitment to safeguarding valuable assets in a cybersecurity landscape that demands vigilance and innovation.

Chapter 12: Physical Security

12.1 Data Center Security Measures

Data centers house an organization's most valuable assets—data and sensitive information. Protecting these facilities from physical threats is crucial to maintaining integrity, confidentiality, and availability. Key security measures start at the perimeter with robust fencing and surveillance systems. Installing motion detectors and security cameras can deter unauthorized access and provide real-time monitoring. Access control systems, such as biometric scanners and keycard entry, ensure that only authorized personnel can enter sensitive areas. It is equally essential to conduct regular security assessments and drills to prepare the staff for potential threats. Environmental controls like fire suppression systems, climate control, and redundant power supplies are vital in protecting hardware and data against environmental threats. By securing the physical premises, data center operators can significantly mitigate risks that could lead to data breaches or equipment failure.

The integration of physical security with cybersecurity efforts creates a layered defense, known as defense in depth. This approach ensures that if one layer is compromised, others still protect the critical assets. For example, even with the best cybersecurity software, if a malicious actor can physically access the server room, they can bypass electronic protections. Thus, physical security measures should encompass everything from the layout of the data center, where sensitive systems are housed, to the protocols governing employee access. By fostering collaboration between the physical security and IT teams, organizations can create a comprehensive threat model that considers both physical and cyber threats. Regular training and updates on the latest security protocols ensure that all personnel are aware of both forms of security, which reinforces a culture of security awareness.

Employing an effective data center security strategy not only minimizes risks associated with physical threats but also enhances the overall cybersecurity posture of the organization. Understanding the interplay between physical and cyber defenses is critical for security professionals aiming to design resilient networks. All measures should be regularly reviewed and updated to adapt to new threats. Continuous improvement, staying informed about emerging security technologies, and collaborating with experts in both fields can further strengthen defenses. Keep in mind that enforcing strict security policies and maintaining awareness of best practices are just as crucial as any technological solution.

12.2 Employee Security Training

Employee training programs are crucial in today's fast-paced digital landscape where human errors pose significant risks to security. The reality is that even the most robust firewalls and advanced security systems can falter if employees are not adequately trained. Recognizing the human element in cybersecurity is essential. Organizations often overlook the fact that a well-meaning employee can inadvertently become a weak link by falling victim to phishing attacks or leaking sensitive information. By fostering a culture of security awareness through thorough training programs, companies not only empower their workforce but also create an environment where vigilance is second nature. Regularly updating these training programs to address emerging threats ensures that employees remain informed and prepared.

Effective training approaches for raising security awareness involve integrating varied methods to engage employees fully. Interactive sessions that include simulations and real-world scenarios can significantly enhance understanding while maintaining interest. Workshops can guide employees through best practices, and utilizing gamification elements can transform learning into an active and enjoyable experience. Online modules can serve as supplemental resources, allowing employees to learn at their own pace while reinforcing key concepts through quizzes and assessments. Moreover, ongoing communication about security updates and threats ensures that employees remain aware and responsive to changes. Creating an environment that encourages discussion around security topics—perhaps through regular team meetings—can help engrain a collective responsibility towards maintaining security.

In developing a robust employee security training program, it's vital to assess the unique needs of the organization and tailor the content accordingly. Consider conducting a vulnerability assessment or surveys to identify knowledge gaps among employees. This targeted approach not only maximizes the relevance of the training but also increases engagement and retention. Running refresher courses periodically helps reinforce the training material as cybersecurity is an ever-evolving field. Finally, encourage employees to report incidents or potential threats without fear of reprisal, fostering a transparent environment where learning from mistakes is welcomed. Building these practices into a solid training program can significantly reduce vulnerabilities caused by human error.

12.3 Environmental Controls

Maintaining a secure data center involves far more than the latest firewalls or intrusion detection systems; environmental controls like temperature and humidity are critical components of system integrity and security. Fluctuations in temperature can lead to overheating of servers, which may cause hardware failures, reduced performance, or even unexpected shutdowns. Over time, these conditions can lead to costly downtimes that can cripple operations and expose sensitive data to increased vulnerability. In this context, effective cooling systems not only preserve the functionality of equipment but also protect against potential data breaches that can occur when systems overheat or operate outside of their specifications. The very act of monitoring and controlling these environmental factors signals to stakeholders that an organization values not just security, but the reliability of its infrastructure, which can instill confidence in clients and partners alike.

The relationship between environmental conditions and hardware reliability cannot be overstated. As components within servers and networking equipment endure prolonged exposure to unfavorable conditions, their operational lifespan diminishes. High humidity can lead to condensation, which poses a risk of short-circuiting or corrosion in critical components. Conversely, excessively low humidity may result in static electricity build-up, which can be equally damaging during maintenance or equipment handling. Implementing a robust environmental monitoring system allows for real-time feedback on conditions within the data center, enabling timely interventions that can mitigate risks associated with both extreme temperature and humidity levels. Security professionals need to integrate these controls into their overarching security policies, recognizing that safeguarding physical assets is as crucial as defending against digital threats.

Cybersecurity is an evolving discipline, and as security professionals strive for a defense-in-depth approach, they should not overlook the role of environmental management in their strategies. Regular training for personnel on the importance of maintaining optimal environmental conditions and establishing strict protocols for monitoring can create a culture of preparedness. It's also beneficial to leverage advanced technologies such as AI-driven environmental controls that can predict and respond to changes in conditions automatically. This step not only enhances security but also streamlines operational efficiencies, demonstrating that a proactive approach to environmental controls is paramount in fortifying a resilient data center.

Chapter 13: Security Governance and Compliance

13.1 Developing Security Policies

Strong security policies serve as the backbone of an organization's security strategy, providing clear guidelines that govern how an organization protects its information assets. These policies are essential not only for compliance but also for establishing accountability and setting expectations around the security responsibilities of all employees. A well-crafted security policy helps in creating a culture of security awareness, ensuring that every team member understands their role in safeguarding sensitive data. Such policies also act as a reference point during security incidents, guiding the response process efficiently and minimizing potential damage. Therefore, investing time and resources into developing strong security policies can significantly bolster an organization's overall governance and risk management framework.

Creating, implementing, and maintaining effective security policies requires careful planning and execution. Best practices recommend starting with a thorough risk assessment to identify critical assets and potential vulnerabilities. This assessment should inform policy development, ensuring that the policies address relevant threats and align with the organization's overall objectives. Once a draft policy is created, it should be reviewed by various stakeholders, including legal, compliance, and operational teams, to ensure that it meets all regulatory requirements and practical considerations. After finalizing the policy, effective communication is vital; all employees should be trained on the policy, and the rationale behind it should be clearly explained. Regular reviews and updates of the policies are crucial, as the threat landscape is constantly evolving. By establishing a routine process for revisiting and revising security policies, organizations can adapt to new challenges and continuously strengthen their security posture.

Incorporating feedback mechanisms can further enhance the effectiveness of security policies. Encouraging employees to share their experiences and suggestions can provide valuable insights into the practical application of these policies in real-world scenarios. Additionally, using metrics to track policy adherence and incident response can help in evaluating the effectiveness of security measures and guide future adjustments. Understanding that security is not a one-time effort but an ongoing commitment can foster a proactive approach to risk management. This mindset is crucial when designing networks with a defense-in-depth strategy, ensuring that multiple layers of security are not only in place but are also continuously assessed and improved upon.

13.2 Compliance Frameworks

Compliance frameworks play a crucial role in the landscape of security management. Among the most recognized frameworks are NIST (National Institute of Standards and Technology) and ISO (International Organization for Standardization). NIST offers comprehensive guidelines through its Cybersecurity Framework, which emphasizes a risk management approach. It helps organizations identify, protect, detect, respond, and recover from cyber threats. Meanwhile, ISO 27001 provides a systematic approach to managing sensitive company information, ensuring its security through an Information Security Management System (ISMS). Each framework has its specific purpose and methodology, allowing organizations to adopt practices that align with their needs, regulatory requirements, and industry standards. Understanding these frameworks not only aids in complying with legal obligations but also enhances the overall cybersecurity strategy of an organization. By leveraging these guidelines, professionals can better assess their organization's current maturity level and implement necessary changes to strengthen their defense mechanisms effectively.

The significance of compliance in establishing trust within an organization's security posture cannot be overstated. When companies adhere to well-respected compliance frameworks, they signal their commitment to maintaining high standards of data protection and risk management. This commitment helps foster trust among stakeholders, including employees, customers, and partners. By meeting or exceeding regulatory requirements, organizations can demonstrate transparency and reliability, which are essential in an era where cybersecurity threats are increasingly prevalent. Moreover, compliance mechanisms often include regular audits and assessments, creating a culture of accountability and continuous improvement. As security professionals design networks with a defense-in-depth strategy, the integration of compliance into this framework not only reinforces the security architecture but also builds confidence among users that their data is being handled responsibly and securely. By cultivating an environment of trust, organizations can improve their reputation and ultimately support business growth.

For security professionals, understanding and implementing compliance frameworks is not just about checking boxes; it is about creating a resilient security culture. Continuous education on these frameworks coupled with practical application will empower professionals to design networks that not only comply with regulations but also foster an adaptive security posture. Engaging in hands-on assessments, collaborating with teams across various departments, and discussing compliance initiatives can deepen knowledge and expertise. Such efforts contribute to a robust defense in depth, protecting critical assets against ever-evolving cybersecurity threats.

13.3 Auditing and Assessment Methods

Conducting security audits and assessments is crucial for any organization aiming to maintain compliance with industry regulations, standards, and best practices. A commonly used methodology includes the Risk Assessment Process, where security professionals identify assets, assess vulnerabilities, and evaluate the potential impact of threats. This process typically involves gathering information through reviews of policies and procedures, interviewing staff, and checking logs. The focus should be on understanding how these elements fit into the overall security framework of the organization. Applying frameworks like ISO 27001 or NIST SP 800-53 can also guide the audit process, helping professionals align their assessments with recognized best practices for risk management and information security. Regular penetration testing and vulnerability assessments complement this by providing real-world insights into an organization's security posture through simulated attacks, which help identify weak spots that need to be repaired or strengthened.

Various tools and techniques enhance the security auditing process and provide a systematic approach to evaluate the defenses in place. Common tools include vulnerability scanners such as Nessus and OpenVAS, which automate the detection of security flaws across networked systems. Additionally, configuration management tools like Chef or Puppet are invaluable in maintaining security standards across devices throughout their lifecycle. For log management, tools like Splunk or ELK Stack can analyze network traffic and system logs, making it possible to detect anomalies that could indicate a breach. Conducting a thorough audit also involves leveraging frameworks like the CIS Controls, which provide a detailed set of cybersecurity best practices to implement and assess. Furthermore, tools for automated compliance assessments, such as security ratings services, continuously monitor an organization's security stance against industry benchmarks. Utilizing a combination of manual techniques and automated tools ensures a comprehensive approach to security audits, facilitating a proactive security environment.

When designing networks with defense in depth, it's essential to remember that auditing is not a one-time activity. Regularly scheduled audits are key to adapting to evolving threats and compliance requirements. Maintaining an agile approach to security auditing, including periodic reviews of both automated and manual procedures, enables organizations to evolve alongside the cybersecurity landscape. This ongoing commitment to assessment enhances the organization's resilience and can significantly reduce the risk of security breaches. Encourage a culture of continuous improvement where security practices are revisited and refined, and stay informed about the latest advancements and methodologies in the cybersecurity field to ensure that your defense strategies remain effective.

Chapter 14: Future Trends in Cyber Security

14.1 Emerging Technologies and Their Implications

Emerging technologies like blockchain and quantum computing are redefining the landscape of cybersecurity. Blockchain provides a decentralized method of storing and sharing information, which can significantly enhance data integrity and authenticity. When implemented properly, it allows for immutable records that can reduce fraud and unauthorized alterations. These qualities of blockchain are particularly valuable in sectors like finance, healthcare, and supply chain management, where data breaches can have severe repercussions. Additionally, the concept of smart contracts enables automated enforcement of agreements, minimizing human intervention and, consequently, the risk of human error. However, while its advantages are substantial, blockchain is not immune to threats. Cybercriminals are increasingly targeting decentralized applications, necessitating robust security measures to protect against vulnerabilities inherent in their design.

Quantum computing presents another layer of complexity to the cybersecurity landscape. Its ability to process vast amounts of data exponentially faster than classical computers raises questions about traditional encryption methods. Algorithms that were once considered secure could be rendered obsolete, as quantum computers possess the capability to break current cryptographic methods through techniques like Shor's algorithm. This reality places immense pressure on organizations to seek quantum-resistant algorithms and adjust their cryptographic schemes accordingly. Understanding how these technologies could be exploited is essential for cybersecurity professionals who wish to stay ahead of potential threats. It is crucial to actively monitor advancements in quantum computing and blockchain technology to proactively adapt security measures, ensuring robust defenses are in place before vulnerabilities are exploited.

To effectively incorporate these emerging technologies into existing security programs, cybersecurity professionals need to embrace a strategy of continuous learning and adaptation. One critical approach is to conduct regular assessments of the organization's infrastructure, identifying integration points for blockchain and quantum technology. This may involve upgrading existing systems to support decentralized application frameworks or implementing new encryption standards designed for quantum resilience. Collaboration with experts in blockchain and quantum computing can also enhance the security program, providing insights into industry best practices and emerging threats. Equally important is the fostering of a security culture within the organization that emphasizes awareness of these technologies, ensuring all team members understand both their potential and their pitfalls. Continuous training and workshops on emerging technologies can elevate the competency of the cybersecurity workforce, enabling them to design networks with a defense-in-depth strategy that remains effective in the face of evolving threats.

As you move forward in designing networks with a multi-layered security approach, keep in mind the importance of regular penetration testing to identify weaknesses in your system. This proactive method can help you understand how emerging technologies interact within your infrastructure and where you might need to reinforce your defenses.

14.2 AI and Machine Learning in Security

Artificial intelligence (AI) and machine learning (ML) are fundamentally transforming the field of cybersecurity by enhancing threat detection and response capabilities. These technologies enable organizations to analyze vast amounts of data quickly and accurately, identifying potential threats that may go unnoticed by traditional security measures. For instance, AI algorithms can sift through logs and network traffic, spotting anomalies that indicate malicious activity. By learning from historical data, these systems become increasingly effective over time, adapting to new patterns of behavior that may signify an imminent attack. When integrated into security operations, AI and ML tools can assist cybersecurity professionals in prioritizing threats based on their severity and potential impact, thereby optimizing incident response protocols. The use of such advanced technologies can greatly reduce response times, allowing teams to address emerging threats before they escalate into significant breaches.

While the potential of AI and machine learning in cybersecurity is immense, several challenges and ethical considerations merit attention. Implementing these technologies requires not only substantial financial investment but also a commitment to ongoing training and maintenance to ensure systems remain effective against evolving threats. It is crucial to consider the accuracy and bias of ML algorithms, as incorrect data or flawed models can lead to false positives or negatives, ultimately undermining trust in the system. Moreover, the reliance on automated decision-making raises ethical concerns about accountability and transparency. As AI systems increasingly influence critical security decisions, addressing these ethical dilemmas is essential to maintain public trust and compliance with regulatory frameworks. Cybersecurity professionals must strike a balance between leveraging cutting-edge technology and ensuring their implementations are ethically sound and inclusive.

As you explore the integration of AI and machine learning into your cybersecurity strategies, consider starting with small, manageable projects that allow you to evaluate the effectiveness of these technologies in your specific environment. Assess your existing infrastructure and identify areas where automation can alleviate manual workloads while enhancing threat detection capabilities. Continually invest in education and skills training for your team, ensuring that everyone is equipped to work alongside these advanced tools effectively. By fostering a culture of continuous learning and critical examination of the ethical implications, you can navigate the complexities of AI and machine learning deployment while greatly enhancing your organization's cybersecurity posture.

14.3 The Role of Automation

Automation has the potential to significantly streamline security processes and enhance overall efficiency within an organization. By leveraging automated tools, cybersecurity professionals can reduce the manual effort required for various tasks, such as monitoring network traffic, managing alerts, and performing incident responses. Automation can handle repetitive tasks like log analysis or security updates, allowing professionals to focus on more strategic aspects of their roles. For example, Security Information and Event Management (SIEM) systems can automatically aggregate and analyze logs from multiple sources, quickly identifying anomalies that may indicate a security breach. This not only speeds up detection times but also minimizes the likelihood of human error, which can often lead to critical oversights in security protocols. Furthermore, automating risk assessments can lead to more consistent evaluation methodologies, enabling teams to respond proactively rather than reactively to potential threats.

However, while embracing automation in security decision-making can lead to improved efficiency, it is essential to consider the implications of depending heavily on automated systems. One significant concern is the possibility of over-reliance on these technologies, which may result in diminished human oversight. Automated systems, no matter how sophisticated, can be susceptible to false positives or negatives, and without proper human intervention, these inaccuracies may go unaddressed, impacting the overall security posture. Moreover, decisions made by automated systems can lack the nuanced understanding that human professionals possess, particularly when contextual understanding plays a crucial role in assessing security situations. Therefore, it is imperative to strike a balance between automated processes and human expertise. Regular reviews and audits of automated systems are necessary to ensure they function as intended, adapting them to new threats as they arise while keeping professionals engaged in the decision-making process.

To adequately balance automation in security processes, organizations should implement a hybrid model where automation supplements and enhances human capabilities instead of replacing them. This approach not only increases efficiency but fosters an environment where security professionals can interpret data with greater context. It is beneficial for teams to engage in ongoing training focused on how to best utilize automated tools while maintaining critical thinking skills. By developing an integrated strategy that combines the strengths of both automation and human insight, organizations can effectively create a robust defensive posture in their network security design, ultimately fortifying their defenses against increasingly sophisticated cyber threats.

Chapter 15: Case Studies and Real-World Applications

15.1 Successful Implementations

Organizations across various sectors have adopted Defense in Depth strategies with remarkable success, illustrating the effectiveness of layered security measures. One notable case is a major financial institution that faced significant threats from cyber criminals looking to access sensitive customer information. By implementing a multi-layered security approach that included advanced firewalls, intrusion detection systems, and regular security training for employees, the organization succeeded not only in preventing breaches but also in enhancing its overall security posture. This layered strategy helped create redundancies, so even if one layer was compromised, others would still protect the organization's data and infrastructure.

Another exemplary case is a healthcare provider that integrated Defense in Depth to meet stringent regulatory requirements while ensuring patient data safety. They deployed a combination of endpoint security solutions, data encryption, and robust access controls. The experience revealed the importance of continually assessing and updating security measures to adapt to new threats. By conducting regular security audits and encouraging a culture of vigilance among staff, the organization not only secured patient data but also fostered trust among patients and partners alike.

From these real-world applications, several lessons emerge that can inform the practices of other organizations. One key takeaway is the importance of situational awareness; understanding the unique threat landscape that pertains to an organization is essential in determining which layers of security to prioritize. Furthermore, involving all stakeholders—from IT staff to executives—in the security strategy development process enhances buy-in and promotes a security-minded culture. Ensuring that defenses are not just a checkbox exercise, but an integrated part of the organization's ethos, can make a significant difference in resilience against attacks. A practical tip for cyber security professionals is to continually engage with industry forums and threat intelligence resources to stay ahead of emerging threats and refine defense strategies accordingly.

15.2 Lessons Learned from Breaches

Analyzing well-known incidents of cybersecurity breaches reveals a pattern of failures across various security layers. Take the case of the Equifax breach in 2017, where attackers exploited a known vulnerability in the Apache Struts web application framework. Despite a patch being available for months prior, the organization failed to implement it, demonstrating a critical lapse in their patch management process. This incident not only compromised the personal data of approximately 147 million individuals but also highlighted the necessity of maintaining an updated inventory of software and ensuring rigorous adherence to patching schedules. Another poignant example is the Target breach, which involved the infiltration of their network through a third-party vendor. The attackers gained access to point-of-sale systems, leading to the compromise of 40 million credit and debit card accounts. This breach underscores the importance of securing the supply chain and implementing strict access controls for third-party relationships. Each of these incidents reflects the multifaceted nature of security failures where neglecting even one layer can lead to significant repercussions.

Drawing actionable insights from these breaches emphasizes the need to refine Defence in Depth strategies. A critical takeaway from the Equifax breach is the imperative of robust vulnerability management and timely application of patches. Organizations should adopt a proactive approach to identify and remediate vulnerabilities within their systems, incorporating automated tools that can streamline this process. Furthermore, the Target incident reinforces the necessity of scrutinizing third-party vendors thoroughly. It is essential to establish a rigorous cybersecurity assessment framework that evaluates the security postures of all partners and vendors regularly, ensuring that they adhere to your organization's security standards. Additionally, integrating network segmentation can help contain breaches, limiting lateral movement within the system. By creating zones that restrict access to sensitive data based on user roles, organizations can mitigate risk significantly. Learning from past failures and adapting these insights into actionable strategies can bolster an organization's defense mechanisms, fostering a resilient cybersecurity environment.

Regular training and simulations for employees also emerge as a crucial lesson. Enhancing awareness of potential threats can mitigate human error, often at the core of many breaches. Incorporating a culture of continuous learning and preparedness will empower personnel to recognize and respond effectively to security threats. Fostering adherence to best practices in cybersecurity hygiene across all levels of an organization ensures a more robust defense. For a practical tip, creating an incident response plan that includes defined roles and responsibilities can streamline actions in the event of a breach. Regularly testing this plan through simulated attacks will ensure that your organization is not only aware of potential threats but is also well-prepared to defend against them.

15.3 Best Practices in Defence in Depth

Implementing Defence in Depth requires careful consideration of best practices that have stood the test of time in various industries. Industry leaders emphasize the importance of layering security measures across all levels of an organization. For instance, while a robust firewall is essential, it should not be the sole line of defense. Businesses are encouraged to employ multiple forms of security such as endpoint protection, intrusion detection systems, and data encryption. Understanding the unique threats that your organization faces is vital; therefore, conducting regular threat assessments alongside continuous monitoring can help formulate a well-informed strategy. Integration and collaboration across various security tools can enhance the overall effectiveness, creating a synergy that strengthens network security. Developing a strong organizational culture around security awareness is also crucial, empowering employees to recognize and report threats effectively. Ultimately, the best practices highlight that security is a continuous process that adapts in response to new vulnerabilities and emerging attack vectors.

For cybersecurity professionals looking to strengthen their organization's defenses, adopting actionable strategies is key. Begin by conducting a thorough audit of existing security measures to identify any gaps or vulnerabilities. Leverage segmentation to isolate critical assets, preventing attackers from easily accessing sensitive data, even if they breach external defenses. Implement robust access controls with the principle of least privilege, ensuring users have only the permissions necessary for their tasks. Regular training sessions to keep all employees informed about security best practices can significantly bolster your defenses. Additionally, invest in automation tools that can quickly respond to threats, allowing your organization to react faster than potential attackers. Using threat intelligence can stay ahead of new methods attackers may use, making preemptive actions more feasible. Maintaining regular software updates and patch management further secures endpoints against exploitation. Remember that cyber resilience involves continuous improvement; establish an iterative process where lessons learned from incidents feed back into your security posture.

Utilizing the right mix of technology, policy, and user awareness will create a robust framework for Defence in Depth. Embrace the idea that every layer should complement one another, allowing for an interconnected, responsive security ecosystem. Regularly reassess strategies based on changing threats and business operations to ensure their effectiveness. Keep in mind that defense strategies should evolve and that the cyber landscape is perpetually changing, making ongoing education, investment, and a proactive mindset indispensable for long-term success.

Chapter 16: Conclusion and Next Steps

16.1 Recap of Key Concepts

Defence in Depth is a multi-layered approach to security that emphasizes the necessity of using various defensive strategies to protect information and technology assets. Throughout this book, we explored fundamental principles such as identifying the assets that require protection, determining the threats and vulnerabilities associated with them, and implementing several overlapping security measures that can include firewalls, intrusion detection systems, encryption, and access controls. Every layer in this strategy serves a distinct role, working together to mitigate risks and provide a more robust security posture. The understanding that no single security solution is foolproof underlines the importance of integrating various tools and practices to create a comprehensive defense mechanism against potential breaches.

As we continue to navigate an ever-evolving cybersecurity landscape, the importance of continual learning cannot be overstated. New threats and vulnerabilities emerge constantly, challenging even the most rigorous security setups. Professionals must engage in regular training and stay informed about the latest developments in technology and cyber threats. This ongoing education can take many forms, including attending workshops, reading the latest research, actively participating in cybersecurity communities, and even pursuing professional certifications. By fostering a culture of growth and curiosity, cybersecurity professionals can ensure that they not only protect their current environments effectively but also anticipate and adapt to the changes and challenges that the future holds.

To stay ahead in this dynamic field, always seek to deepen your understanding of emerging technologies and their implications for security. Practicing hands-on skills, testing out new tools in controlled environments, and collaborating with peers can sharpen your expertise. Incorporate regular assessments of your knowledge and skills to identify areas for improvement. Cybersecurity is not just about implementing solutions; it's equally about a mindset of vigilance and adaptability in the face of continuous change.

16.2 Continuing Education in Cyber Security

Cybersecurity is an ever-evolving field, and the need for continuous education is paramount for professionals looking to stay ahead. With the increasing sophistication of cyber threats, there are numerous opportunities for further education and professional development. Online platforms like Coursera, Udemy, and LinkedIn Learning offer courses that cater to various levels of expertise, from foundational principles to advanced topics. Many universities now provide specialized degrees in cybersecurity, which can deepen your knowledge and credibility in the field. Additionally, workshops and conferences can be invaluable for networking and learning about the latest trends and technologies. Participating in these educational opportunities enhances not only your skills but also your career prospects in an industry that rewards knowledge and adaptability.

Certifications play a crucial role in establishing professional credibility, particularly in areas like Defence in Depth. Programs such as Certified Information Systems Security Professional (CISSP), Certified Ethical Hacker (CEH), and CompTIA Security+ are designed to enhance your understanding of multilayered security strategies. These certifications provide rigorous training and coverage of essential concepts like access control, network security, and incident response. Completing courses with a focus on Defence in Depth equips professionals with the knowledge required to implement a multi-layer security approach effectively. Some organizations may even offer internal training programs that allow employees to prepare for specific certifications while gaining practical experience in their everyday roles. By investing in these certifications, cyber professionals can create robust network designs that protect against an array of attacks.

For those practicing Defence in Depth, it's beneficial to integrate knowledge from various domains, such as risk management, compliance, and incident response. Cybersecurity is not just about technology; it's also about understanding the business impacts of threats. Engaging with resources that emphasize real-world applications, such as case studies and simulation exercises, can give you a more comprehensive view of how to design and implement effective security measures. Keeping abreast of new tools and best practices is essential, as is fostering a collaborative environment where knowledge sharing is encouraged. Explore mentorship opportunities, and consider joining professional organizations like (ISC)² or ISACA that focus on member education and professional development in cybersecurity. Continuous learning and professional growth are not just advantageous; they are essential in navigating the complexities of modern cyber threats.

16.3 Building a Career in Defence in Depth

In the ever-evolving field of cybersecurity, a multitude of career paths exists for professionals interested in Defence in Depth strategies. These paths include roles such as security analysts, network architects, and incident responders, each playing a critical role in protecting organizations from an array of cyber threats. Security analysts focus on monitoring and managing security incidents, while network architects design robust network infrastructure with multiple layers of security. Incident responders handle breaches and formulate strategies to mitigate future risks. Along with these traditional roles, there are specialized positions like penetration testers, who assess vulnerabilities in systems, and cybersecurity consultants, who provide expert advice tailored to individual organizations. This broad spectrum of job functions highlights the importance of gaining expertise in Defence in Depth, as it encompasses the creation of a security architecture that integrates multiple layers of security controls across the IT environment. Developing a strong foundation in secure coding practices, risk management, and threat modeling can substantially increase your marketability in these roles.

Networking and mentorship are vital components for professional growth in cybersecurity. Engaging with experienced professionals in the field can provide invaluable insights and advice, paving the way for learning new strategies and best practices. Consider joining cybersecurity-focused organizations or local chapters of professional associations, as these platforms often host events that facilitate meaningful connections. Online forums, webinars, and social media groups dedicated to cybersecurity are rich with opportunities to engage with mentors and peers. Seek out professionals whose work resonates with your goals and reach out for informal discussions or shadowing opportunities. Many experienced cybersecurity experts are willing to share their knowledge and may even guide you through the complexities of career advancement. As you build your network, be proactive in offering your skills or knowledge as a way to create balanced relationships. Remember that mentorship is a two-way street and fostering these relationships can lead not only to self-improvement but also to collaborative opportunities that enhance your career in Defence in Depth.

Staying current with the latest trends and emerging technologies in cybersecurity is crucial for any professional aiming to excel in the Defence in Depth arena. Participate in training programs, obtain relevant certifications, and attend industry conferences to remain competitive in this dynamic field.

Engage in continuous learning, whether through formal education or self-study, as this not only enhances your expertise but also demonstrates your commitment to the field. Building a career in this area requires dedication and a willingness to adapt, so embrace change and remain curious about the multitude of cybersecurity advancements. Offer to lead projects or initiatives within your organization that focus on implementing Defence in Depth principles, as practical experience significantly strengthens your resume and showcases your skills to future employers.